Planets

Written by Kim Jackson

Illustrated by James Watling

Troll Associates

Library of Congress Cataloging in Publication Data

Jackson, Kim (Kim J.)
  The planets.

    Summary: Simple text and illustrations introduce the
nine planets of our universe.
    1. Planets—Juvenile literature.   [1. Planets]
I. Watling, James, ill.   II. Title.
QB602.J33   1985   523.4   84-16451
ISBN 0-8167-0450-3 (lib. bdg.)
ISBN 0-8167-0451-1 (pbk.)

10 9 8 7 6 5 4 3 2 1

Our world is a planet.

Our world is a planet named Earth.

Nine planets move around the sun.

Our sun is not a planet.

It is a star!

Our sun gives us heat and light.

Planets close to the sun are very hot.

Planets far from the sun are very cold.

A planet named Mercury is closest to the sun.

Mercury is very hot!

A planet named Venus looks bright.

From Earth, Venus looks bright, like a star!

A planet named Mars is red.

Mars has two moons!

A planet named Jupiter is very big.

Jupiter is the biggest planet.

A planet named Saturn has rings.

The rings are made of ice and rock.

A planet named Uranus also has rings.

Uranus has rings and five moons!

A planet named Neptune is far away.

Neptune is almost too far for us to see.

A planet named Pluto is very far from the sun.

Pluto is very cold!

Our planet Earth is just right for us.

Maybe someday we will visit the other planets.

Which planet would you visit?